Themes of my life

Also by Roger Brown:

The Truth Seeker's Handbook
Heading Out
Encounters
Insights
33 Years of Dreams

THEMES
of my life

from the
Truthseeker's Handbook

Philosophy and Introspection coalescing into themes, addressing some of the core issues of life...

Roger Golden Brown

Golden Galaxy Publications

Only the road and the dawn, the sun, the wind, and the rain,
And the watch fire under stars, and sleep, and the road again.
- John Masefield

Introduction

I was born to a British mother and a father whose family tree goes back to the 1500's in America. I grew up in the woods, north of Seattle. I was raised a Quaker. My father was an inspiration in every sense, a spiritually oriented man of high integrity. Also my entrance onto the Earth scene was timed to be someone born to be at the heart of the hippie movement and to contribute to helping the world change for the better. I was also born an Aquarian. And I embrace that as I identify physically as a world citizen and spiritually as a player in the greater scheme of things.

I have lived in many places, done quite a potpourri of work, and have known many unique individuals. Amidst the variety that spiced my life an integral part of a significant period of time was writing in journals. This started on San Jaun Island in Washington State in 1975. Through good times and hard times I wrote almost daily for over 20 years, recording observations, thoughts, feelings, dreams (both the nighttime and the aspirational varieties), and experiences; both physical experiences and some more etheric experiences.

Life is a trip. Amidst the uncertainties, during this journey, I have tried to at least be aware of what is going on around me and what is going on within me. Using entries from my journals and elaborating on them, I have put together writings that make up this and other books.

So… fellow sojourner. Welcome.

Themes

Throughout the 97 volumes of journals that I have filled there are various thoughts and observations and epiphanies that I have had that seem to recur. They arise in many different contexts. And they take many different forms but over time and with ongoing reflection, they seem to have coalesced into themes that I have found to be cogent and helpful.

Contents

Honesty

This theme is just a primer on some basic principles of honesty and the virtues - no, on the functional necessity of honesty. I believe it underlies virtually every learning tool on the road to heaven. The ability to learn from mistakes, the act of forgiving, any community or team or friendship efforts, or a personal confidence that will endure - all rely on honesty or they will inevitably go awry.

- - -

As the world is shrinking faster and faster I feel a sense of optimism. Although I am discouraged often with how people behave, I see ultimately how the growing closer will lead to union.

I call it the tower of lies. When you lie, you create a structure that needs supporting by more lies. Who hasn't discovered the difficulty of not telling the truth and had to keep covering their tracks with more fabrications. For this structure to sustain itself it must have a place to hide the truth. One method is to blame someone else or discredit someone or some information, so that a conflicting story can't damage the preferred story. The problem with this is that it requires dark areas, secrets, and enemies. Enemies who we can say want to distort the truth for their own wicked agenda.

But as information and communication systems become more and more available, dark areas cease to exist. And with the ease of travel and even the exposure of television, we have learned that even in the countries led by "bad guys" the people are not vermin. They cry for their families and children too.It's slow; denial is a powerful technique to ease the pain. But slowly the truth will out. The tower of lies gets more and more rickety as it gets higher and higher. The stresses increase and eventually it collapses.

- - -

You can only tell so many lies before it's clear that it doesn't make any sense. When you're dishonest you're forever trying to figure out what is going on. If everyone was straight and honest we would know what was going on. Be honest, be real, know where you stand. Ultimately, honesty is the path of least friction. The truth always dovetails.

- - -

Yes, we must be honest. With my tower of lies analogy, I was mostly addressing the societal realm. But honesty is equally, or perhaps more important in our personal relationships. Don't dissemble and smooth things over. That smoothness is an illusion. Tell it like it is. We may lose friends but we'll surely gain others and bring a higher grade into our lives. If the truth drives someone or something away from you, then what did you have anyway? Imagine a world where everyone was honest. We'd all know what each other wanted. It would be so much easier to help and to solve problems.

What's more, honesty must be more than just not lying when directly confronted with something. It must be sharing with the intention of helping each other understand so all involved can be clear.

- - -

And if we truly hope to interact with others with honesty and integrity we must first be fully honest with ourselves. Being really truthful and open is how one finds oneself into the beauty that unfolds. Just like growing a flower or a fruit, love is the agreement with natural law. If you use poisons or try and manipulate the system, you spend energy forever trying to manipulate it back into order. Loving and open honesty are the keywords of spiritual ecology.

- - -

In life it is often beneficial to seek balance. Regarding honesty, however, it's not necessary to seek the balance. Truth and honesty are pure in and of themselves, not needing a balance. It's the honesty of our actions that gives the balance.

- - -

From the book, Illusions: "Your conscience is the measure of the honesty of your selfishness." Now what the heck does that mean, you might ask.

It's so simple, really. Unity is the source of pleasure. When we are "together", we are unified within ourselves, and can easily fit without. Like if you are "centered", "together", "home", you can see clearly out. To not be honest, to not act in confidence, to fear and consequently to try and manipulate outcomes, you accede to satisfy the needs of the armor, the responses to protect us from the assaults on ourselves from past experiences. Then it's like being a bent piece and trying to fit in the puzzle. Honesty and selfish confidence are the candles for the yet to be illuminated new frontiers outside the armor.

If we can shuck the guilt that says it's not ok to be selfish, if we are honest about our selfishness, our power increases; our intent becomes more unified, and we become more effective. Paradoxically, our conscience would be clearer to give "unselfishly."

- - -

A short story about honesty:

During a time when I was building massage tables for a living, I learned a valuable lesson with the aid of a good friend. I had just finished a table and noticed a teensy hole in the vinyl. It really bummed me out. I didn't know if I should let it go or tell the clients who were coming over to buy it.

My friend Ken called and I mentioned it to him. He said that we often try and guess people's reactions and don't give them credit and usually imagine worse scenarios than what would probably happen if we were open. The situation, the problem/possibility, was that two women were coming over together for two tables and since I only had two tables done, one would have to make a compromise.

Well, I told them and it was a bit of a dilemma but the humor was good and I offered possibilities; to redo it or give a reduction, maybe 5, 10 or 15 dollars. I left the room and left them alone and when I came back they had decided who would take it for $15 off. It was good vibes all around.

- - -

Delight in truth at all costs.

We really must accept everything we experience. Simply say, yes, this is happening to me. We tend to avoid and repress and choose against less pleasant feelings. What a rip-off! They offer powerful information as to what is going on; information as to the reason why we don't at the moment have pleasant feelings. The desirable feelings validate flow and rightness. The unpleasant ones are the ones needing the most attention.

- - -

This journal entry is a great example of this:

> Tonight my ear hurts. I'm asking myself about it. I was tempted to say, "what is wrong with my ear?" How awful. If one must think in terms of "wrong" a more accurate and helpful approach would be to ask, "what's wrong with my truth?" More accurately, "what's lacking in my truth that my ear is alerting me to?"
>
> It's your basic: If you do it right, it's gone. If you do it wrong, it's still there.
>
> What part of myself, related to this ear pain, (pain = alert) is being held out of harmonious flow in denial? Which is to say out of consciousness.
>
> You have to bring things into consciousness out of their lairs into the light.... then let them, with awareness, slip away out of consciousness.

- - -

I conclude the honesty theme with a sub-theme:

Reality is Synonymous With Power

On deeper levels honesty must also include a dedication to validating all that we think and all that we feel and all that our senses perceive. This fits in with what I said about "information" and the tower of lies. All information is good information. Don't blame the messenger. We must validate all that we perceive. Anything less leads us on a wild goose chase. And leaves us open to the mass hypnosis of the planetary paradigms; not to mention the powerful norms of every little clique a person may associate with. A true measure of friendship would be the amount of allowance and even encouragement one offers another to explore a reality that is engendered by their own thoughts, feelings, and senses.

- - -

Some of my favorite lines from the Doors are in this final stanza of the song, Strange Days.

- - -

Strange days have found us
And through their strange hours
We linger alone
Bodies confused
Memories misused
As we run from the day
To a strange night of stone

- - -

Bodies confused, memories misused. Think about what is being said here. When any information is distorted to fit into some kind of preconceived idea, it leaves the body confused. If someone feels sexual desire but their religion tells them that such feelings are bad, it will certainly confuse the body. If pain or discomfort is masked by drugs the body is cheated out of the information it needs and the natural biofeedback it needs to take the best path to healing itself and to learn for future similar situations.

If someone feels greedy, but because of some spiritual belief that tells them that they should feel all-giving and one with all, they might suppress it or camouflage it and they will have installed a memory that is false. If someone feels abused by a friend, but feels that the friendship means too much to be compromised by bad feelings, they may convince themselves that it wasn't really like that in an attempt to soften the conflict. And, of course, there are the basics like denial and justification, pretending something really didn't happen or inventing reasons for feelings or acts so they don't go against a self image, or whatever style is perceived to be one's own.

When you are running your life and trying to modify your behavior, no matter how good your intentions are, if you are drawing on memories that aren't real; that aren't honest, then you are traveling a muddy road. It's the old how can you get to where you'd like to go if you don't know where you are. You are running "from the day to a strange night of stone." Where there could be light and self-improvement, although possibly challenging, there is darkness and rigidness.

Yes, reality is synonymous with power.

- - -

Endeavor to not cheat yourself out of reality, out of your own reality as you mingle with and communicate with people who do not want to know the true nature of things; who would happily gloss over the awkward. It's ok to share but stick up for your reality, at least remain aware of it.

It might seem that this might leave you lonely or separate from those whose small talk avoids the complexities (and with it, the beauty) of the human condition. But this is not true. Paradoxically you may find that relationships will become easier when you're not trying to accommodate others people's worlds by altering you own perception of reality. Just say, "here I am, here's what I see, you can take it or leave it." You have nothing to hide because you've got nothing to alter. You are at your best.

This from my journals:

> A couple of nights ago I was thinking about Gina and phantasizing being close to her and thinking how my feelings really would want her, even though I know any phantasy of continued togetherness is pretty inappropriate. Not the phantasy (nothing inappropriate there), but the reality of acting on it, I mean. Which is the point. I recognized that as my will and wisdom become more capable I can allow myself to recognize real feelings, because I don't feel afraid that I'll act inappropriately on those feelings. I can allow myself to feel lust for women who are too young or too anything to actually get involved with. I can allow myself to feel anger towards someone without having to "do" anything about it. And on and on. And what that does is allow me to better let these feelings flow, to observe them freer of bodies confused and memories misused. They can play themselves out undistorted.

When intense feelings would compel a person into destructive or radically challenging acts, I think those feelings are suppressed to avoid that. Keeping as much as possible of the current reality of your life validated helps you become clearer and gives more room for past baggage to come back which can now be handled and released, in the light of reality.

- - -

As one becomes freer and clearer, the honest pictures, unfiltered and undiluted can come out and be learned from. Bodies will not be confused and memories will not be misused. I can entertain phantasies and I can allow all thoughts and urges conscious awareness because I have less and less guilt about the implications of that. I have more and more faith in my ability to behave lovingly with consideration for higher spiritual concerns and golden sharings and allowings. And more and more ability to feel it, let it go, and release as I go.

Guilt is a big reason why people get muddled. It's why people need law. They don't trust themselves to behave. Guilt is like that internal law. "I can't (allow myself to) feel that. If I feel that without guilt, if I let myself have, or worse, enjoy that feeling, just think of what horrible things I might do."

But it's a short term solution. And suppressed, those feelings will eventually explode and manifest in confusion, distress, or disharmonious behavior.

- - -

Let me repeat:
How can you get to where you'd like to go if you don't know where you are?
The truth always dovetails.
Delight in truth at all costs.
Reality is synonymous with power.

Hoax

It was near the winter solstice when I went to see Brother Sun, Sister Moon, the beautiful Zeffirelli film. I was deeply moved. Saint Francis had given up the life of a wealthy family to help others and spend his life in service. Clare, the woman he loved, stayed behind continuing her life as it was.

Later in the film after she has had an epiphany, she finds him and says to him, "I don't want to be loved anymore, I want to love. I don't want to be understood any longer, I want to understand."

I left the theater feeling a determination to open to loving; to really know I have something to give.

- - -

The desire to really prioritize giving and loving really came home to me two months later. It had been getting a bit springish in Santa Cruz where I was living at the time, and one special day it was in the 80's with a luscious wind blowing off the mountains.

A part of me woke up. I would call it an epiphany except that it was too native and too much of the body, too much embodied in me to call it anything like a realization. It was a knowing.

I went out into the day and felt such a rush of love; physical as well as emotional. I could feel my hands tenderly aching to give. My breathing was from the depth of my gut. I spent the day, first at home, then outside in the country and finally in town among my fellow gods, rushing, drunk on longing to love.

Yes! It's all a big fake.
Perpetrated by those of low confidence,
by those who feel little.
The hoax that we need to be loved.

- - -

It's easy to get stuck in the fear to admit that we are Great enough and Full enough to love so beautifully; that our real need is to give love. To run it. To flood it out onto fellow humans.

We've got to believe that we've got something to give.

What is it to be human? Whether it is from the oxygen we breath in or the energy showered upon us by the cosmos, or simply the stuff of life bestowed on us at birth, energy is life. Energy comes in and energy goes out. We are, in effect, a transmitting station. The thing is to decide; to feel if it goes out in pain or if it goes out in art, if it goes out in hate and fear or if it goes out in loving.

As Wilhelm Reich said regarding this, "It is really the only question. And the one that is never asked." Going into Wilhelm Reich now would be out of the scope of this writing but a main theme of his deserves some mention. And that is that when you draw your energy in, in fear, you contract. When you send energy out, in love, you expand. And this expansion is the essence of what enriches life giving us health on all levels.

- - -

There have been times when I have caught myself caught up in the flux of emotions relative to daily life and I have felt myself wanting to be loved; wanting love to come to me. Not feeling enough within. It's not an altogether good feeling. There is a human richness to it but it also feels weak. I would suggest that at such times simply try and live what grace you can here and now and work work work on keeping the energy and love energy flowing out and not give into the hoax of trying to draw things towards yourself.

I admit to neediness. But there have also been times when I felt that I was enough within to give, not needing anything coming back. And it is a clean feeling of power. At such times one thing I have noticed that accompanies this feeling is that I feel no sense of being a victim and no sense of self pity for what I don't have.

But let me be clear that in recognizing the hoax and that the highest energy is to be giving love, there is no conflict between that and the receiving of love. In fact, the expansion and openness when one is giving allows love in more easily than when we feel needy and contract. There is also a bit of a paradox here. And that is that when you can fully receive, free of any implications; when you can just simply take it, then you know, really know, what giving is and that it's worth it. Recognize and accept the gifts you are given as part of the whole. Then complete the circle. Circulate that energy back out into the world.

- - -

The following is an excerpt from my journals; a bit of struggling with believing in the hoax but feeling stuck:

> What is recognizing my power and purity; my good intentions? And what is selfish? And how much selfishness am I entitled to? Can't I do (be) both?
>
> Maybe it's just that if I'm looking for physical ends, I need to employ physical means. Without diluting or cheapening my spiritual quest, I need to be equal in my validation of my physical quest. Be of unified heart; of unified mind; of unified application of self. It's all one package. I'm all one package.
>
> That also means taking a physically realistic look at where I want to be, where I am, and how to play the game. "Realistic" meaning how it works now; whether it is a social or a personal paradigm.
>
> I'm reminded of one of the basics that recurred often in the Edgar Cayce readings. "Bring your ideals into your personality." Maybe that is the bridge between spiritual ideals and physical "needs."

\- - -

The iron stove story; how the hoax works socially as well:

My friend and roommate Michael wanted to build a hot tub and use a wood stove to heat it. I had noticed an old iron stove in an alley while bike riding and a couple of days later I went by and asked the owners about it. They gave it to me. It was in good shape and all the parts were there.

When I went, it was just to get it for Michael, but when I got it and checked it out I felt greedy and wanted to keep it or sell it or something.

But I felt kind of bad about that and when I brought it home, I told Michael that I felt a little greedy about it and it might fit in my sauna (which currently had a stove in it). He didn't seem to understand what I was trying to say and after we looked at it, said "thanks", mistakenly accepting it as a gift.

Any greed I had had disappeared in the next couple of minutes. It just felt good to let it go and pass it on and have it used. I felt clearly and cleanly how that facilitates a tight knit functional economy. A tight knit functional energy output, production, use, time, effective economy.

Capitalist communism.

Objects aren't owned collectively and shared by legislated order. It's just that if we function as a team, there isn't surplus clogging everything up. Privately "owned" objects, (as much as one can own anything) are given up like feeding the open player in basketball.

\- - -

I can't get out of the Hoax theme without at least a passing mention of sex.

Hungry for sex, once, I realized very clearly that satisfied doesn't mean getting sex; it means getting fulfillment or completion in some way; feeling unity and loved and loving.

When these needs aren't met the desire for sex serves as a means to satisfaction. Not that sex isn't a part of that satisfying. Just that it will never be the solution. And I think when one is unsatisfied and feels that charge, it is so primal and therefore immediate that it takes wisdom to keep attention on our real needs.

- - -

While it's natural to want and to hope to get strokes for accomplishments and to receive love and attention, instead realize that "results" such as successes and failures are all part of the whole. And the more you participate and the more that you are an active agent for the greater good, then what you might have seen before as a success, you now recognize as a part of the flow and part of the bigger picture.

Perhaps what might have been seen as a highlight, is now seen as an integral part of the light.

- - -

Finally, I would say that believing in the hoax doesn't mean that acting as a channel of giving love is as simple as reminding oneself. The paradigm of getting and accumulating and requiring is pervasive. Just try and keep your eye on the prize: love as an organic all-inclusive comprehensive way of life.

Acts are best done in the spirit of giving, not as a duty but as our birthright and because it is the essence of health on all levels; done in the spirit of unity. "Success" is not an isolated over and done with tangible thing, but rather the smooth functioning of the whole.

God and Participation

Yesterday was cool! I rounded a corner, took a breath, saw a yellow rose (generally my favorite color by smell), and a butterfly fluttered by. I noticed the trees didn't just blow in the breeze, but shimmered. Clouds weren't just in the sky. They hung there, gently morphing.

It was like Rod Serling's Twilight Zone. The surroundings are the same but something has changed. You've entered the Twilight Zone.

In my case I felt I'd entered the God Zone.

Visually, things had nice crisp edges. And like a good nostalgia trigger, smells had a crisp edged quality to them.

But, paradoxically, they somehow, kinda, sorta, hung together as one. (Maybe as "One." Big "O".)

I looked up. It just seemed I should look up. So I looked up in the sky and I saw God (That's where God is, up in the sky, right.) I think it's just because when you look up you look out and when you look down you look in. Though I have noticed that if you look far enough out you're looking in again.... but that's a different story.... Wait a minute. Maybe that isn't a different story. That is this story.

But it wasn't really only in the sky I saw God. (Yeah. Big "G" God.) It's like we're in the Milky Way but you don't see it just glancing to the right or left. No, you look far out you see it in the sky and we're hangin' on the edge.

It came to me. So clearly. Simple really; clear crisp edged thoughts and ideas that, however, weren't limited. Maybe an epiphany is something that seems like it should be, used to be, and maybe "normally" is weird... but now not. It's fantastic, but it's right where and when it's supposed to be. "However humble, there's no place like...."

God.

At that moment the idea of God was not difficult or mystifying or mystified. It wasn't only for the religious or the devout. God is…. well, …. I could see at that moment that God cannot be defined in terms of anything in time, space, or matter as a definitive being. I saw that as one gets more in tune, thinking and acting more in unity, one gets closer to God and the closer to God one gets the more the separation begins to break down and God and the beholder approach unity. There would be no ego separation that could or would (even if it was desired, which I'm sure at this point, it wouldn't be) distinguish God as a specific form or being. The relationship is dynamic. I used the words "closer to God." It's more like more integrated.

Edgar Cayce, the great psychic, in one of his psychic readings, described God as being within oneself first, then manifest outside, as all of our's God. The Universal Mind.

Certainly we've all heard many variations of "we are all one" and "God is everywhere in everything."

Perhaps the idea of a single entity "God" is not incompatible with this. Perhaps, we do all, indeed, as the truest form of God, combine to form a Universal Mind or spirit. But here on earth there are very few of us humble souls who are free enough to reach a high level of unity that supports a fully integrated Universal Mind, especially when we are wrapped up in our daily life concerns and agendas. But, the Universal Mind is made up of all consciousness, not just human and earthly, and in spite of the relative insufficiencies of most of us, it has incredible integrity and power. So, to us, it would appear to be a unit, a single being, an intelligence, a mind, or a spirit that is all knowing and holy. It is not apart from us; it is simply a part of us; the purest center and concentration, seen from the outlands.

- - -

And how do our actions, the acts we carry out, fit into the idea of unity. It's like a player in a team sport who feels no sense of disappointment at not having had a chance to make a particular play when a teammate makes it and succeeds for the whole. The feeling is pure support for the action which successfully benefits the whole.

And as you act for the team you realize that expectations or demands for personal recognition or rewards put on life or the universe must be transcended. Instead of thinking in terms of personal success or personal rewards you now simply recognize accomplishments as a facet of the "everything" that you participate in.

You have just moved a little bit closer to the center of God. Or, if you prefer, you have moved a little closer to complete union with "One." I struggle with words here to not put anyone off. You get the picture. Find your own words. Or perhaps, if you can feel it without words, you're even closer.

- - -

Influenced by reading the book Right Use of Will talking of always loving yourself unconditionally, I told myself over and over to do so and looked around at myself and others and tried to see everyone as gods, kind of roaming around on earth. Since then it has been very powerful for me to see my fellow sojourners as little gods roaming around, interacting, emoting, sharing. I believe this is a really powerful way to look out at the world; maybe because it is really true. We are all divine and equal as spirits. Here is me in a journal entry seeing people this way:

> In the co-op this evening I was in a really serene state, looking at people in various ways attractive to me and often really looking and feeling, moving on and actually laughing at.... I'm not sure.... laughing at their beauty?, in my freedom?, the gentle way they carry on?, seeing people as little gods, kinda milling around, weaving individual acts into what it is on this planet.

What I find interesting is how positive the whole picture was that I described. Beauty. Freedom. These qualities are natural to us all and even when we find things to be critical about, it is helpful to remember that we are indeed little gods and all contributors to the universal mind and a greater God.

- - -

And there is a personal element related to the participation aspect of getting closer to the center of God. Reflecting on the paradox of as you get to know yourself better, you are more able to sense yourself as a part of the whole and in unity with all, I saw clearly how that makes sense. You might think that putting energy into getting to know yourself would make you more into separateness but actually what is happening is that lots of energy and behavior and responses that aren't yours are removed and that leaves you clearer in your role as a dynamic vital participant. Which is different than a togetherness with little or no personal soul searching because when programmed responses dominate your behavior you are in one respect more together with others – intertwined - but it is your mucky psychology and dominating, need to control side that is interacting. This explains also the perspective of the 1st chakra family tribe nation love that moves people so deeply; the patriotic attachments that make people feel so much attraction to one person while having animosity for others who are different. It's a bad dance. Free of that programming, the chemistry gets better and better.

So it is important that we must be a participant at all levels. Be aware of ourselves as gods in the greater scheme of things and be aware of ourselves as imperfect individuals increasing our self awareness in order to function as smoothly as possible.

Evil

The word evil is such a hot word and a real button for many people. It sounds so dark and it is so often used as an absolute. In conversations it can really set people off. Visions of Hitler or slavery arise. Some don't believe in it at all and others believe we are all evil, while still others believe they are not and certain other people or groups are inherently evil. But I maintain that evil is not one fixed state of being that is reserved for the most dastardly people. It is an element of life as a human. And it exists in many different amounts in each person. Also it is not an absolute within any one person. A person may act in an evil way under one set of circumstances and not under another. Or under one set of circumstances at one time, and then not under similar circumstances at another time. What's more, I think one needs to be clear that evil is not the opposite of good.

It may be easier to just look at the world as good guys and bad guys but that insults the potential we all have to deal with the complexities of the human condition.

- - -

So, what is evil by my reckoning?

I read a friend of mine a dream I'd had about being obstructed by evil souls and she took exception to the concept of evil. I said I viewed it simply as the other end of the spectrum from harmony. And that now I do believe in evil beings; simply as those whose pain and solitude is so intense that they will do anything to anyone to keep from having their hoax exposed; to keep from having to face themselves.

But I believe I should modify the above. That is too absolute. There is no pure evil. It's all relative. Intensely evil might dominate and abuse huge amounts of people or mildly evil might just be willing to ruin your day to mask some pain. And within any being evil or lack of it is not absolute. It depends on the moment. Life is after all a series of choices.

My friend answered me in saying, "but it wasn't intentional and if it's not intentional, it's not evil."

I said certainly it is intentional. It is unconscious, but intentional, none the less. The choices she and I make every day with awareness are buried many layers down for many people. And within the limits of our enlightenment we too probably take actions to protect ourselves from exposing our weaknesses; that with which we are out of harmony. And, it is true, in every part of the spectrum, people seek to control others for their own validation. I guess that's really a challenge to try and not coerce any one in order to support our insufficiencies. And to be aware when we do.

- - -

In another dream I was trying to define evil. It was very specifically explained. Here are the words I used in my dream. "Whenever, whoever doesn't allow anyone, anytime to do what they want." But I was uncertain about the "to do what they want" part and tossed around alternatives like "freedom." Struggling with the end went on a long time.

When I wrote it down it seemed like me telling me to allow everyone their own path. Which is also me telling me to allow me my own path. It's circular.

- - -

Also I would go so far as to say that there are no evil thoughts. Only evil acts. On this stage on earth we are here as souls to learn in the physical plane, where we choose to manifest impulses physically. And grow and improve ourselves depending on our choices.

In the original Star Trek TV series there was an episode called A Taste Of Armageddon in which, when Kirk destroys the machines that sanitized their war, the people were horrified of the possibility of facing the true ugliness of war.

Kirk gave the following soliloquy:

"War is instinctive. But the instinct can be fought. We're human beings with the blood of a million savage years on our hands! But we can stop it. We can admit that we're killers ... but we're not going to kill today. That's all it takes! Knowing that we're not going to kill ..... today!"

So the thoughts are there. Do we act on them and create disharmony? Or do we rise above the impulse for the betterment of ourselves and all around us?

- - -

Although I said that there are no evil thoughts, only evil acts, there is inner turmoil generated by lack of willingness to take life and its complexities on without imposing your will on others. Hate is one such manifestation of this turmoil. And although hate is not in and of itself evil, if not dealt with within, it can often lead to evil manifest.

I once had a clear realization about reasons to hate.

It came clear to me that people don't have reasons to hate. They just want to hate and find reasons to justify their hate. If the plantation owner didn't have the niggers to hate it would be his wife or neighbor. If the redneck didn't have the hippie to hate it would be his boss or the guy who sold him some shoddy merchandise. If the hippie didn't have Nixon to hate it would be the neighbor's dog or the weather.

And it came to me that we can look at levels of justifying hate as a barometer of our growth and enlightenment. And we can (and do, on some level of awareness) use that barometer to constantly be letting go of baggage (becoming en-lighten-ed), continually changing the filter that finds "good" reasons to justify hating whatever it is that you hate.

This helps cleansing the self of justification for acts of evil and, of course, helps us move closer to the center of God.

- - -

It seems clear, looking at the spectrum of individuals this way, that truly no acts of aggression or "evil" are personal. They are simply acting and reacting in fear response with emotional baggage.

And there is a connection between how people hurt other people and/or hurt the environment. Everybody does what they think gives them power.

Here's an example of that. The other day, my brother was telling me how some loggers, for a demonstration against the environmentalists, drove their trucks around and how crude it seemed to him.

It struck me how perfect it was. That's where they get their power. A person with more faith in the ether might stand quietly with a candle, because that's where they get their power. Or at least, in both cases, where these people think or believe they get their power. I realized that essentially that's what we all do, to some extent all the time; everything we do, every act. We do what we think gives us our power, brings us our power, leads us to our power.

That doesn't seem to explain how often we, as humans, seem to waste our power or choose paths of denial and avoidance of positive responsible behavior.

That's the trap. We might waste time or act out physically in ways that fall short of our ideals or seem to exhibit a real lack of introspection, but that is us choosing the shortsightedness of the avoidance of the pain or discomfort of acts that challenge our status quo. Avoiding a challenge and the struggle to overcome the way we are can seem to give us more power than the outcome of the struggle would ultimately give us.

And perhaps the challenge in all growth and spiritual unfoldment is to recognize as a learner, or show, as a teacher, that the result of taking on challenges and breaking through will lead to a kind of harmony and flow and trust and faith that really does increase our power.

- - -

I want to wrap up this section on the evil theme with a story of an example of evil manifested by good people with all good intentions. At the time the incident struck me as being in essence very similar to the concept of fascism, assuming the right to control others, believing themselves to be superior or authorized.

I looked up fascism and came up with this definition:

> Any movement, ideology, or attitude that favors dictatorial government, centralized control of private enterprise, repression of all opposition, and favors extreme nationalism. The most notable characteristic of a fascist country is the separation and persecution or denial of equality to a specific segment of the population based upon superficial qualities or belief systems. Simply stated, a fascist government always has one class of citizens that is considered superior (good) to another (bad) based upon race, creed or origin.

Now, although this definition defines fascism in terms of a government, the concept applies also to individuals whose actions dominate others. The story:

Some years ago I built and sold massage tables. One day a woman I knew, Annie, came over with a massage therapist friend Jenni, to look at my tables to maybe buy one. The following is the excerpt from my journals:

> Somehow the subject of doing massage without a license came up with me maintaining that why should anyone need the government's approval to choose to pay anyone for a massage. It was a major button for them. Jenni said it's a good thing that massage therapists must be licensed. She had her reasons. Shoddy arguments. They both said, as the conversation developed, that it was very

complicated. God, how simple can it be. Choice. Freedom. No victims. She said it was simpler in a state where a license is required; she's not called up for sex. It's like an ad in Penthouse I once saw, about censorship. Yes, now your life is a lot simpler and a little less free.

I explained the Profound Simplicity of choice and she couldn't get past the fear. She was worried that somebody messing with your energy who doesn't know what they are doing could be really bad.

Regarding my views, Annie said they were so idealistic. Yeah, so what?! If not us, who? If not now, when? Haven't we slaughtered and dominated enough for enough centuries, millennia because adults have concluded that ideals are teenage stuff and not attainable in, they say, the "real world."

I'll sit at your round table, Arthur.

It was just amazing hearing Jenni defend a small group of people's right to legislate their ethics. She defended it saying it wasn't the government; it was a group of massage therapists.

God, every fascist state will tell you their experts know best and should decide the standards. Who cares who they are? Who decides who gets to decide?! There are no victims. It really is that simple.

It was weird too. I felt very harsh talking my talk. In the face of their resistance, my concepts were an affront on crystallized concluded battle lines of right and wrong. In a healthy sane world it would have been reversed. Her imposition on my freedom would have seemed very harsh indeed.

The paradigm and hypnosis of fear. It really is the essence of evil. Fear that a world of choice by individuals taking responsibility for themselves is too dangerous and we need control by authorities to protect us.

And how freely and without the simplest critical thinking it is assumed that a particular group of people have a bead on what is right and best and safest and, most importantly, necessary.

It hurts to meet intelligent, caring, sensitive people who just can't see the simplest of freedoms. Choice, victimless crimes.

One more thing. If someone sees the logic and truth in freedom of choice but still thinks we need controls and limits, I ask again:

Can it really be that we live in a world where doing what is right, won't work? It's all so clouded in complex scenarios of tragedy, but it really is so simple.

It comes back to my definition of evil. That battle line of right and wrong is determined by fear. When the light (of reason, of truth) begins to compel a person to face their denials but threatens to compromise what they perceive as their security, it is at this point, if the light does not prevail, where they begin to need to control their environment, abusing and dominating others (beings, creatures, nature) to protect their lie and avoid having to deal with complexities and their personal inner struggle.

- - -

And finally, something else that ties in with the idea of people controlling others. And that is that one of the biggest problems in the world is that people don't believe that doing what is right will work, when in fact it is the only thing that will work. In this case a dominant social paradigm is reinforced by those who lack vision and/or faith.

You hear it in religion, you hear it in politics, you hear it socially. "Yeah, that would be the ideal thing to do but it won't work in the real world." People are forever accepting destructiveness, inequality, and compromises to integrity because they don't believe that doing the right thing will work. And the paradigm is reinforced and feeds itself and makes the right thing ever more incompatible with *their* real world.

As a friend of mine once said, "anything that isn't value oriented, is doomed to failure."

Committee Members

I had an experience once with a person with whom I had been very close and who had expressed her interest and excitement in our friendship, then for no reason apparent to me, decided that it was altogether too challenging, and that even to talk became "impossible."

A friend shared something with me that gave me great insight into why we meet such inconsistency in people. Each person has a committee in their heads. Each moment behavior is dictated by inner (not necessarily conscious) decisions made by this committee. Each member of the committee has their own voice and agendas and priorities. And when the final decision is reached it may compromise a previous decision about a seemingly similar situation. It may not resemble a previous presumed reality closely, or at all. This can occur with complete unawareness that this has happened, consequently completely befuddling another person who this decision is being communicated to or who it may affect.

- - -

In life we register information through our senses. And being the mental animals that we are, we usually use the mind to evaluate this input. When we do this we have options, choices. What is it that is building our mind? Where do our opinions come from? What drives our decisions? First hand experience and information, or information reviewed and censured by a committee with an agenda? Or what blend?

- - -

Any conclusion by the committee will depend on when, under what circumstances, and for what reason a consensus is sought. Such a conclusion may be needed to base an action on or it may be to form an opinion.

Here are just a few examples of things that may affect the weight of the committee's voices and the final conclusion, opinion, or action that results:

• Is there a matter of physical survival at hand; be it real or imagined?

• Is a top priority in this moment to impress someone?

• Is there a personal history of opinion or action that doesn't want to be challenged?

• Is there a monetary element that might overshadow ideals that one holds?

• Are there ideals that carry so much weight that they suppress responding to a situation effectively?

If we listen for it, we will begin to hear the voices of the committee members in action. We can train ourselves to be aware of them. And as we begin to recognize the individual members and their individual agendas, we will gain insight into their sources. And also learn to recognize the issues that each member is concerned with and at what times or under what circumstances each committee member contributes their voice.

Also with each inner discussion among these committee members, the issue and the time and the circumstances will shape how loudly each member speaks out and how insistent each is at getting their own way and whether or not they will compromise readily. For every individual their committee members will be unique and the weight they carry in conference will be unique. Childhood experiences, family concerns, health issues and even such things as self image and other pressures put on us by society, friends, family, or self all have a voice.

One other thing that will certainly influence the final outcome is whether in past similar situations, the final decree of the committee lead to a successful or pleasurable outcome or not. Perhaps things have changed enough in one's life so that a choice that failed before will probably succeed now, but there will likely be a committee member who will lobby against taking similar action as before.

- - -

I was feeling anger towards a lover. We were both picking at each other over style concerns. I was disappointed in myself for letting style come between us and ahead of love. This from my journals:

> Though I didn't and really don't now feel it, exactly, it sure seems like another layer of the abandoned boy theme. I still have a voice picking on her for style in my head. I can still hear it as I write this. And that committee member is pouting and throwing a temper tantrum. It's a quiet voice but it's not going to go down so easily, I guess. And I admitted to myself that yes, I blamed over style and that's not good. But even as I write this I hear another voice, this one defending me with pride, "don't back down - blame someone else".

- - -

I'm often disturbed by how easily and effortlessly we glide along in life on a trail of psychological responses. Events compel psychology (That's important. Compel; not cause.) and that psychology surfaces at some later time and off we go in some purely Pavlovian determined direction.

We all have histories and it's not unusual to expect similar results form similar actions. We all have patterns that are innate to us; a style that is unique to us as souls in our bodies in this life. And it's only natural and often helpful that we have learned how to make the best choices for our well-being. But are we making the best choices for our well-being? Are we really being a fair witness or is our mind being made up for us out of awareness by the committee? We have our own ways, but I would suggest that much of what we believe (the committee's final decision) to be our limitations, are not. What we consider to be "me" is not as fixed as one might think. We have free will.

The more in touch we become with our committee members and the more closely we listen in, the better able we will be to help them grow out of being angrily reactionary or pouting or screaming and seeking to control and dominate the group's decision. And the better able we will be to help the whole committee mature and grow in integrity. The trick is to be present at the committee meetings and to take your rightful place at the head of the table.

- - -

Finally, these are some of the committee members that it occurs to me might be contributors to my decision making, personal tastes, prejudices and ultimately action taken, either upon the outside world or shaping my personality:

• I want sex and now under any terms

• I want sex with love and romance

• I want to play hooky

• I want to be responsible and take care of things

• I want to be creative

• I want to it to be perfect – anything less isn't worth it

• I need to make money – I must survive

• I want to make money but under my terms – I must be comfortable

• I want to fit in with people; act in socially acceptable ways

• I must be myself; act as I will regardless of what people
  think

Each person will have their own unique committee with each member having its own relevance to their life and its individual niche in the pecking order of their committee as a whole. Think of the recurring patterns of your life and the choices of your personality and seek to observe and recognize the voices of your own committee members. Consciously become a participant.

- - -

One last thought. Seek to be aware of where each of the committee members is getting their information. Is it from personal experience? Is it from ideas or is it from sensory input? And maybe most importantly, is the information from other people things you haven't actually had experience with but are believing because you "learned" it? It is easy to give a lot of weight to anyone you deem to be an expert or qualified. Be careful or you might find that you have a committee member who is not even part of your home team.

Consumer Consciousness

The level of attaining and consuming and holding onto physical possessions in our culture and especially in these modern times is an addiction and a distraction from other life issues. It is easier (easier in the smaller picture only) to focus on tangible things than to share with each other our real fears and joys. Change is necessary for the human spirit. We choose to experience change outside of ourselves instead of having to deal with it within. And so much effort and attention is put into not just the making of money but the juggling of money required to maintain particular possession standards. And to maintain the possessions themselves. They break down. Our "occupations" are just that. They, rather than living for life itself, take up our time.

- - -

The idea that we live in a culture obsessed with possessions and things is hardly new. But I see the attachment to possessing physical things as only the most superficial and crudest form of consumer consciousness. I believe that it is not unique to the recent centuries in the Western technological cultures or the current spread of ownable objects in the world. It is an extension of the 1st chakra need to claim turf and hold onto it against the world. This is where competition and jealousy and separation and, of course, war ultimately come from.

- - -

But our proclivity towards possessing and holding onto nonphysical things just as one would claim turf comes ultimately from even deeper than any 1st chakra survival consciousness. These are outward extensions of our karmicly compelled choices to hold onto nonphysical things because we aren't ready to let go to totalove; we still feel the need to take a stand against the world personally.

I see this manifested in relationships; particularly in intimate relationships. I have observed it in myself as I have lost a lover to her choice to not be as close to me as she had been. I feel cheated and like somebody owes me something. And I want to "have."

From a journal entry, the continuing conflict between the forces of unity and separation:

> The challenge of being at peace with myself amidst the head trips regarding hoped for futures with and the longing for Lori has compelled me to draw on my wisdom.
>
> The fact that I was feeling so solid within before (which created the space for her to come into my life in the first place) has compelled me to try and not lose the power that has been drawing in such beauty, amidst the drama of the physical world's separating and isolating influences.
>
> It's like a consumer mentality. Such and such desirable happens and you act like you own it (or them) now. If it goes away or changes, how dare that be taken from me.

- - -

Consumer consciousness can be related to things, people, or even conditions; even such things as the weather or a long line in the store. It's all too easy to forget that it is all a flow made up of all the participants and we just have to accept the small piece of the whole we are sharing in at any one moment. We must try and maintain grace and work on allowing the dynamics and not buy into the hoax of feeling we should own such moments in time.

- - -

I have often marveled at the appeal of Ronald Reagan and his happy-go-lucky superficiality; his epitomizing the American Dream. Einstein once said, "Everything should be made as simple as possible but not simpler." The Reagan mentality (and that of his huge following) gains its strength from its blindness to the complexity of the human condition and instead reduces everything to manageable proportions with only denial, self deceit and the suppression of conflicting evidence necessary. This is a case of making things simpler than possible. At least simpler than what is necessary if you want to function instead of decay. This mentality promotes consumption in its most wasteful way.

At times I have looked at people who, in my opinion, were behaving badly and thought of the expression "behaving like children." But that's not fair so I came up with the idea of "indoctrinated children." Unlike the natural beauty of content children, indoctrinated children fight over consumer products and the right of selfish freedom; indoctrinated into the cultural paradigm of individual stockpiling.

This leads to an unhealthy form of competitiveness and the belief that if we work hard enough we can get ahead. The problem is that ahead in this case means ahead of others and as we rise in this kind of competitive world, somebody always has to pay the price and if we want a piece of the action it will need be done at the expense of someone enslaved or downtrodden somewhere.

The paradigm of accumulation as an ideal must be blown apart. Not that having anything is bad but the obsession with it and the prioritizing of consumption must give way to a value based consciousness.

- - -

In this world of G.D.P. (gross domestic product) measuring the productiveness of countries, which seems to conflate production and well being, there has been an alternative idea from the small Himalayan kingdom of Bhutan. In 1972, Bhutan's new leader, King Jigme Singye Wangchuck, decided that in line with their Buddhist spiritual values they needed a different measure than that of western material values. He decided that the measure should be the G.N.H., or gross national happiness. Happiness as the goal to be achieved through development as opposed to development as a means to having more. To this end the king instituted policies and took efforts so that prosperity would be shared across society and that it was balanced against preserving cultural traditions and protecting the environment.

It is only values and other non-possessable "things" that can guide us through the great problems of the world and help foster well being, security and happiness.

- - -

And finally, this journal entry is a good example of me wanting to escape because things had changed. I wanted to own the stability. Struggling with conflicting desires and with my questions about life style and place; with community choices and with climate preferences:

> I had a realization while walking today. It seems important and I hope I can profit from recognizing it.

> The rhythm I had for the month in California before I came up north into the winter is gone. At least its outward appearance and probably both what ways I was given gifts and how I recognize the gifts I was given. I may have, discover, recognize, or settle into another rhythm but that previous particular phase is gone. So many conditions have changed. Both externally and how I perceive things. I realize it would be destructive and wasteful to seek that same rhythm or lament its passing. Now I must simply try and live what grace I can.

34

Physical things come and go. People come and go. Creature comforts come and go. Values and sharing and love prevail if you make room for them. They are our birthright and inviolable. Seek to cultivate them.

True Efficiency

The idea of efficiency has become extremely distorted. In this rat race world, efficiency seems to have come to mean several things which I would say are very shallow minded gauges of true efficiency.

One main measure is time – clock time. Faster is better, often with little regard to quality. Faster, whether it is faster that something is produced or faster that we get somewhere or faster that we can get something done so that we can get on to something else. Which, of course, will also have to be done as fast as possible to get on to something else. That's efficiency.

- - -

When I lived in Hawaii I worked as a checker in a health food store.

Another checker harassed me for being slow and taking too much time with the customers, which really disturbed me.

So I got to thinking, why are people in such a hurry? It seemed clear to me that it's because what they're doing isn't enjoyable. Or it is not felt fully enough and appreciated or valued enough. It's that simple.

Maybe at the store we should have had one line for people who want to chat amongst each other and with farmer Brown while they buy their goods at the market and another line for those people who want to be processed like the numbers on their credit cards, "efficiently," so they can get going and get more done.

Maybe the difference is between the goals of getting things "done." Over and done. Or "doing." Enjoying the process; feeling good along the way. Just what is the point of getting more things done, if none of those things are enjoyable.

I am sure that here someone could argue that some things are rushed so as to have more time for things that are more enjoyable. There is some truth to that but I would say that if that is the case then the overall lifestyle and choices of activities needs to be questioned. And I would also say that to be engaged in a balancing act of rushing through unenjoyable events to get to enjoyable events has a pitfall. The rushing creates stress which will often carry over to the times when we choose to slow down.

- - -

As well as faster, bigger and more are also often thought to be equated with efficiency and productiveness. If one is good, two must be better. If one boogawatt of power production will provide our community well, then certainly two will make life even better and/or easier. I think it is all too often that bigger and more are simply assumed to be desirable and are the goals, and how much bigger and how much more indicate efficiency.

- - -

True efficiency must take in to account all factors. One factor is the consumption of material and energy and everything involved in their being harnessed for whatever is wanting to be accomplished. Another factor is the well-being of all people whose lives are touched by whatever is being done. Another would be the impact of the act or event itself on the person who is supposed to be benefitting from it; not just on the surface if it gets something done but is there value and appreciation. It's like I could work 4 hours doing something I don't enjoy and get paid $80 and then go and spend that money plus $20 out of my pocket to buy a piece of furniture or I could spend that same $20 on materials and spend 8 hours in the shop whistling while I work and build that piece of furniture. Would that be inefficient to spend twice as much time or would the satisfaction of a job well done and the feeling and residual energy of having spent such a pleasant day constitute true efficiency?

Certainly that is for each individual to decide. In this life there is bound to be undesirable things that must be done and choices to be made. But I think one should always look at the whole to decide which route to take.

The same question might be applied to gift giving; Christmas gifts, for example. I could do all my shopping in one day or I might to choose to chip away at several craft projects over a period of weeks and give home-made gifts. The appreciation of the receiver of the gifts and overall warmth of the experience must be considered in calculating the true efficiency.

- - -

I think a little needs to be said here about these times, often referred to as "the information age." The efficiency of the computer is unparalleled. Or is it?

As far as efficiency goes, I believe the experience of going to and spending time at the library to study something or maybe being compelled to try an experiment yourself to get an answer or needing help from friends or a teacher may offer much more than the slick ability of a computer to seek out and isolate the intended item.

I know my life would have been gaunt had the accidents, the wrong turns, and the serendipitous encounters been replaced by the efficiency of targeting a sought out piece of information on a computer. Not to mention that the openness of the mind required to deal with those wrong turns and mistakes offers so much more.

The idea that you can get more information from a zillion items of verbal information coming down a wire than you can, say, from the same amount of time spent looking at a stump decaying in the woods, is ludicrous.

- - -

One of the narratives in politics these days is that now is not the time to spend money on such things as health care as a community responsibility or to invest in new approaches to help the environment; during these hard times we need to stick with the status quo. This is a great example of fragmented shortsighted thinking. While the money machines and the interests of the greedy (and the masses who blindly get behind the program) have foisted themselves and their factories on the world for the dollar made today, no care has been taken to see if they would fit; if the earth could accommodate them. As time goes along the manifestations of these poorly conceived ideas get more and more out of balance. Shortsightedness just leads to forever having to rework that which is out of balance in a patchwork fashion in an attempt to forestall its collapse. This is not efficient. It is upside down.

More on the dollar made today. On a personal level, accumulating money and the leverage it gives us in life make the amount of money we have and saving on bargain purchases seem desirable. It's not that simple. There are many side issues around making more and more money and spending money superficially efficiently that affect the big picture which will come back to haunt us. It is often the case that the ways in which money is made and that which is involved in a "growing" economy has consequences. It is often overlooked that beyond the obvious value of having more money left over today, the money you have may be worth less tomorrow because of your actions. In a similar vein it is extremely inefficient to put your money in a bank, regardless of the dollar made today that they promise you, if that bank is using your money to make people's lives miserable and reduce the quality of life for all of us.

Doing the right thing is always more efficient. There are, of course, times, in a physical world and a manifest world that is out of balance, when less than the most truly efficient routes must be taken back to balance and harmony. But all less efficient steps taken must be acknowledged as such and be taken in awareness.

- - -

I have been eating as much organic food as I can for many decades now. Especially early on, before it became more in vogue, I would have friends say, "yeah, but it's so expensive." My answer was simple. You can pay a little extra for organic food now or you can pay a lot more for doctors later. And this is not to mention one's well-being in the meantime. And this well-being goes beyond just your health, but includes what you have contributed to the public welfare by not contributing to the poisoning of the earth.

- - -

To seek real efficiency and real value, the bigger picture must always be consulted. Also the soul. If some end is achieved faster or cheaper, is that more efficient if it is at the expense of our sensitivities? We are done of the task sooner but have less spirit with which to carry on.

Efficiency must be, by definition, that which is the best for the balance and the harmony of the whole. Good feelings, pleasurable feelings and compatibility must be measures of efficiency. Justice must be taken into account. Values and ideals must be factored in. With true efficiency ease instead of dis-ease will prevail.

Tourist in Life Concept

Once when I was in the airport in London, I was watching the passengers coming off a plane. Among them was a pretty sizable group of Texans. (I'm guessing but the accent and the 10 gallon hats suggested that to me.) They rambled into the airport and instead of any sort of wonder about being in a new or foreign place or any sort of checking out the environment to gauge how people behaved, they just brought Texas with them and were loud and, I thought, quite insensitive.

During my travels I have noted that there is a big distinction between tourists and travelers. Travelers are simply moving among other fellow earth inhabitants of various cultures in this multi-faceted world, adjusting to their surroundings and consequently sharing and contributing to wherever they are and whoever they are with. They are experiencing and learning and growing personally as well. Tourists, on the other hand, never shuck their home persona or their home paradigms, blundering coarsely along contributing little more than money. Certainly the difference between travelers and tourists is not absolute, but I do notice the distinction generally.

- - -

People who have known me are often amazed by how deeply affected I am by a book or a movie or music. There have been times when I have felt such a deep sensitivity and have felt misunderstood. It occurred to me that the concept of the tourist could be applied in so many other ways than just when traveling.

People are, it seems to me, also tourists in art and tourists in so much that they do. When involved in something or experiencing something, they don't shuck their selves in order to truly experience.

When you read a book, is it just a story or do you allow it to reach you and to affect you? When you listen to music is time altered as it becomes an adventure? Or when you look at a painting is it just a picture or can you go into it? An expression that became popularized in the sixties, which probably sprung from the focus and submersion in the moment that was characteristic of the times as well as being enhanced by psychedelic drugs, was "get into it." Yeah, don't just observe. Get into it; participate.

Another example would be to look at what level people participate with nature when they go camping. Are they tourists in nature, bringing along all the comforts of home, smelling the fresh air, to be sure, but not really submitting themselves enough to really be taking part in nature? Or is the camping trip intended to be an adventure in nature with a real choice to allow yourself to be vulnerable to some extent to really feel what it is like there? I would suggest that if you go beyond being the tourist in nature that even that fresh air would take on a new level of richness.

I wrote "vulnerable" above and I think this is maybe the real issue. The tourist experiences with trepidation and is cautious about allowing themselves to be too out of control. Standardized food choices and standardized accommodations are maintained. It is from inside this safety net that they view or look "at" their surroundings. In situations where people leave the routine, they tend to take their "down pat" selves with them as insulation against being affected and consequently challenged.

- - -

I would go even further and apply this to such things as relationships. When you are with others or with a lover, do you really let yourself into it? Are you willing to be vulnerable in order to fully experience? Or do you seek to maintain your own ways to insure that you won't have to change too much or accommodate too much?

- - -

There is one pattern for me in my life that has been frustrating, even though I see it as a strength. I often find it very difficult to get into people's lives. I'm often awkward and uncertain. But once I'm in, I'm relaxed and get along well and it's easy. With women in particular something that has happened a lot is that we come together when one or the other of us is about to leave, has just arrived, or is traveling.

But it's not just traveling; I've noticed how easily I enter during vulnerable moments. When people are tough and really have their thing down I find it so much harder and if I do get in, I find it less than satisfying. When I or a woman are moving, the everyday life thread, the profession, career, patterns, agenda are suspended or loose and I can enter. I've watched myself gain confidence and flirt and move closer; move in to a nice sharing when I sense that.

It fits with the idea about being a tourist in love. Since I don't desire being a tourist in love and really can't be that way, if I don't see a way in, and sense that she just wants me to touch her on the outside, I don't make the adjustments necessary to stay in the "do you come here often?" mode for very long and that's that.

- - -

This from my journals:

> I've always differentiated between tourists and travelers. Tourists being, well.... you know, ... sightseers, outsiders taking pictures and seeing it as if it were a picture - 2 dimensional; going home virtually unchanged. Travelers being fully alive where they are, still living their life, being affected by their environment; knowing and expecting they will be changed by their experiences - full 3 dimensional involvement. Yes, that fits too with my tourist in

love, or tourist in nature thoughts. I want to be a traveler in love. Open up the threads of our lives, let our loves intermingle and let's travel.

I would go further and suggest that this concept could even be applied to personal reflection and introspection. When your senses perceive something and convey it to you, is it immediately compartmentalized or do you allow yourself to accept it out of predetermined programming and allow yourself to be an adventurer in the moment?

- - -

When I was younger and lived in the Pacific Northwest, I would often go out and play sports on wet playfields with friends. Initially I would be reserved about getting wet and muddy. I would avoid falling or diving for a catch. But sooner or later it would happen anyway. Once I was wet and muddy, it all opened up. That's when the fun began.

- - -

A ship is safe as long as it stays in port, but that's not what ships are built for. Leave the port, leave the hotel, leave your self, leave the way it's always been. Allow the adventure in. Let yourself be taken by the river of unchartered experience and participate.

True Love

Once, when listening to the classical station on the radio, the announcer read a quote from a musician who said the most important part of the music is the listener: "We're all trying to reach the listener." Woah, hold on there! I think the finest music is made when the musicians play for themselves. In a similar vein questions about self focus vs. community came into my mind and it seemed so clear. There is no conflict. How would our body function if the liver was trying to perform for some other part of the body and taking its attention away from its task at hand. The key is to be the best you can be and allow others that for themselves. And when actions bring beings into close (recognizable) contact, then bring in awareness and communication toward recognizing each other's roles toward the best functioning (harmony).

The beauty of it is that as you remain your own organ, the smoother you all function, and the more easily energy can flow through and among you. And with this energy comes the feeling of oneness and union and well-being; this feeling is what we all yearn for. Example: I sure don't want to be (or own) a woman's belly, or breast, or voice, or movement. What am I going to do with that? I want what/who she is when she is as much as she can be of all of what she is. I want to feel the velvet that comes from allowing each other to flow. Any effort towards the other is best only to facilitate the other's opening to their own way.

Take it as far as you want. Any way you look at it, it's by increasing each participant's ability to function smoothly, happily, effectively, that we all reap the benefits.

This is True Love.

- - -

I mentioned to a friend once about how being an individualist is part of the American creed. He seemed very cautious, almost afraid of individuality. He commented, questioning whether it is good, being self oriented and away from the whole.

I got to thinking, how would it be if a drop in the ocean refused to evaporate. "I feel it to evaporate. The temperature is right, the pressure is right. But I'm gonna stay here with you guys. I can't go off and do my own thing."

The rivers would dry up and ocean would stagnate.

It seems paradoxical, but to move freely with our own influences as parts of the whole is what really brings beauty and unity to the whole.

Make no mistake about it. Togetherness because of fear, intimidation, or for purely philosophical reasons is not unity. And certainly not if it requires compromise of self or personal values.

- - -

I once encountered a book titled: Must I Change Who I Am To Be Loved By You? The answer is so obvious. Absolutely. All beings must change who and what they are to be alive. Love is change. Love is motion. What's important, though, is that the changing is done organically and dynamically as part of the relationship and as part of each individual's growth; not in order to comply with one or the other's idea of what form the relationship should ultimately take.

I think that describes well the problem I have had in some relationships. I experienced a lot of pain because I tried to match energy with women who needed validation for who they were statically; not for their motion.

Sure, I guess, in the purest sense of the word love, I can love them too; I can love you if you don't change, but not in the sense of being together in an intimate relationship.

And it's not just me. Any two beings that are together, to validate or because of validating their staticness are going to encounter functioning problems.

I can think right off of some of my friends' relationships that I have observed that were burdened by movement problems because change scared them rather than excited them.

I have always recognized that I need movement and change in relationships. I gave away my power often, thinking if I didn't yield to a status quo, I'd lose something I needed. Now, it's just too clear to me that the value in a relationship that resists the dance of the currents and the impulses of life can't compare to a state, single or coupled, that is free to flow and move and change.

- - -

There is a form of "meditation" that, rather than seeking God or some higher spiritual state, focuses on being aware of yourself, your own energy, and coming back home to feel solid and complete within yourself, in order to function more clearly and effectively.

There was a time when a couple of friends and I had done such a meditation and afterwards we were all aware of how crystal clear everything looked. And I began to wonder if that's also why at times women I have been with have looked so good to me when I was feeling very individual, very me. How much better they looked than when I was losing myself in us.

Certainly it seems that it's been true in my love life that lovers look better when I've done some activity that is for me. What a beautiful paradox and lesson for lovers. There's such a compulsion, almost guilt driven, that we should lose ourselves in each other to attain unity. And going even so far as to think that if we don't, then maybe we don't really care. But by remaining separate we retain our ability to sense, to feel, to see crystal clear, and to function creatively.

I really see now, how, for the most part, a really selfish "I don't feel like it now, tough" attitude can be healthy. The times of coming together will be of a higher quality. True love. Yes! That's what true love is. Loving because at that moment it's exactly what you want to be doing and you are doing it the way you feel like doing it.

And, perhaps, the measure of a relationship is how often true love happens; when both people are expressing love creatively and in their own ways simultaneously often enough to satisfy each other.

And I guess that need (to be satisfied) would always be in flux; paradoxically becoming less with the knowing that the other desires to share their true love with you. Which, of course, makes it easier when it's less demanding.

It's the opposite of the viscous circle!

- - -

This entry from my journals:

> The last couple of days I've been feeling it to be lovers with a woman and feeling really impersonal about it. Keith has said a few times how he wants a woman "for a while" and it seemed so impersonal and kind of weird to me. But now I understand. It is a paradox, really, that in a way that is really an ultimate state and a compliment. It's like two people can love so much that the giving doesn't require any particular response or any particular niche for the other person to fit into or prove anything in order to love. Just love, as freely as they are capable, share, and know it is just that.

- - -

And the true love theme wouldn't be complete without:

Free Love

While playing some romantic 60's songs, I was thinking about my pain and loneliness and my attachment to certain women in my life. I thought about the Prince Valiant and Lady in distress syndrome; about putting them on a pedestal and losing perspective; losing touch with all the elements that constitute objective reality. And how these things create conditions, really create the environment from which my feelings come, or perhaps through which they are filtered, shaped, and charged, coming from deeper within.

And what I came to is this: I believe that in a natural society with joyous, free, spontaneous, creative people, people would receive enough loving. Men and women would flirt, play, and come together easily. In between, or perhaps among, magical relationships of duration, men and women could kiss, could stroke each other, could praise each other, and could make love to each other. With clarity and good intentions various levels of closeness happen naturally.

I feel that if one always knew that loving and appreciation and touch and sex weren't far away, that we wouldn't distort our perceptions to satisfy our need to feel loved or to pretend anybody is more or other than they are.

Of course, this requires participation. Both with each other and with ourselves.

Not having attachments doesn't mean not having commitments.

Without having all your eggs in one basket you can love each other for what you offer in real functional life - not fantasies.

So.... I believe in this. And why doesn't this happen? Very few people are ready for this, which is simply to say they can't imagine it. I can. And I feel in light of this, that finding and/or creating a community or circle of people who desire this is very important to me.

Not a frivolous free love sex society, but a commitment to owning our feelings and owning our emotions. Also a climate where people feel safe to take emotional risks.

True loving.

Life Between and Behind the Lines

While listening to the Doors I was listening to a guitar solo and was thinking of how descriptive the 60's expressions were. "Get into it" is kind of cliché, but that's what I was doing with the guitar solo. I was getting into it. Kinda getting smaller, going into slow motion and microscope size and going inside, until the parts got bigger compared to me.

These lyrics are from the poem "The Movie" on the Doors album "American Prayer":

The program for this evening is not new

You've seen this entertainment through and through

You've seen your birth your life and death

You might recall all of the rest

Did you have a good world when you died?

Enough to base a movie on?

There is something there - an attitude - that is really important. And that is that the real history of the world is lurking between the headlines and the deadlines. Like the essences that are so hard to grasp and that deny form and that are so important and that we belittle because we want, we desperately need to associate with things we can hold on to. Yes, we do all have lives that contain enough to base a movie on. And maybe our task in life is to recognize and validate the guts of our life that just doesn't get much press but has tremendous value. It almost seems to me that finding that could be the key to happiness.

- - -

Get into it. Get past the cliché. Really get into it. Get inside. Slow time down and get in step with whatever you are doing, seeing, hearing, feeling, smelling, touching, or imagining. And validate it all. Be in the center of your life.

- - -

My sophomore year in high school I had an English teacher who had a recurring class discussion theme that was the question, "What is a full life?" There we were, a bunch of 16 year olds who he'd gotten to start thinking about and talking about what we thought a full life was. Can a 16 year old rightly reflect on a full life? Why not. Life is doing; not done.

In today's world especially, I would say, there is pressure to have some sort of notoriety; to do and accomplish things that you can put in your life résumé or post on your personal bulletin board. And there seems to be certain traditional societal standards that define those things that we give recognition for when seen posted by others.

- - -

There has, I think, been some awareness of and improvement regarding this on some levels. For example more has been written in recent years about history from the viewpoint of everyone involved; not just the winners and those with the coarse leverage to effect outcomes of events; not just the (mostly) men who were on the front lines, at least the apparent front lines, making the most noise. But it needs to go further than just giving praise to the less than famous people. We need more validation for the much subtler influences that shape life.

Yes, history is not so simple as a series of acts that you can put your finger on; those acts that lead to laws, leaders, and lands changing in one event or at one distinct moment. There is always a fabulous, multidimensional, rich tapestry of underlying influences.

If some person is famous for something they said, did, discovered, or invented, it would be nice to be able to look back and into their life and see what a spouse might have said or shared with them or what kind of state of mind they were in because of their children. The point is that this is really where the stuff of life and the stuff that shapes our lives come from. Between the lines. And somehow, recognizing the thread is important. Not so much recognizing it in your head as something you can label but recognizing it as the real substance of life.

- - -

The 1967 movie Camelot affects me deeply each time I see it. King Arthur's vision of a new order: not Might makes Right, but Might for Right. And a Round Table. Equals. But as real life takes place, dreams and ideals are challenged by history's weight. Even as King Arthur himself was willing to allow and forgive and to let his heart guide him, the pressures from without were too much.

(If you still have yet to see the movie and don't want some of the essence of the movie and a scene at the end given away don't read this. Rent the movie, watch it, then read this.)

In the end sides are taken and preparation is made for war. A young boy, maybe 11 or 12 years old, has stowed away with the soldiers and reveals himself to King Arthur. He wants to join the battle that is expected at daybreak. The failure of the dream of Camelot and the reverting to the old ways of solving conflict is weighing heavily on Arthur. But in the boy he sees hope; the hope of the future. Yes. There will come a time. Arthur tells him that fighting for Right is not what it's about. He tells the boy to go back and take with him the vision of Camelot as it is in its ideal. And to grow tall and straight and to live for that. He sends him off into the predawn mist and tells him, "Run, boy, run! Behind the lines.

Yes. Go back and keep the dream of Camelot alive. Run, boy, run. Behind the lines!"

Yes. Behind the lines. While all the mayhem and hoopla and futile destruction takes place, run.... behind the lines. And keep the dream alive.

- - -

Reading the Free Press, an alternative newspaper, one day, I really sensed that behind the lines the movement is of such a higher quality. The enlightenment and hopefully the subsequent appropriate enacting is so much deeper and broader. It's not just the apparent event, not the events that get distilled into simple manageable situations that can now be spoken of and worked on, but it's the essence of issues and the unifying principles which is where the guts of movement and change really is.

This entry from my journals:

> Last night I was feeling pretty low. Grim, I guess you could say. As I laid down in bed I became aware of a part of myself, behind the lines, kinda bopping and groovin' to music; being silly and kinda free. Nice to see and realize those feelings are really a part of me; really of part of the whole me.

What do we give press to within ourselves? Is it the struggles that make good news and are easily tapped and accessible? Or is it that which is happening behind the lines of our outer personality? This is where the lodes and loads of gold lie.

Karma and Grace

Every choice is karma.
Every choice is group mind.
Every choice is the earth's aura - the ether.

- - -

There was a time when I was living in the country outside of Santa Cruz, California. It was my habit to work in my outdoor shop at home during the morning and early afternoon. An interesting thing that seemed to have much to do with my waking in and being surrounded by only nature for the first half of the day was that often when I went to town and first saw people at a distance from my car, I saw them as animated shells and saw the choice of each individual to inhabit their own particular handicap; each having brought that with them or actually as them.

I would often be aware of and sense the field of energy around people that is the matrix that protects, no, that holds them to the experiences they have. Like, it's amazing that we don't all have accidents, stub toes, step on nails, etc. much more often. Accidents and events don't just happen. I was "seeing" the field that we each have, somehow linking our bodies to our design. And this is one aspect of the package that we bring into this life as our karma.

- - -

While traveling in Austria, I was offered a place to stay after offering to help an older woman struggling with a bit of carpentry on her house. While there, at one point, she asked about my beliefs. I said I talked to God and to angels, but didn't believe in God as a man. It was conforming with natural law. She agreed.

I explained also how I felt, like the Bible says, we can ask and we shall receive. We can look for signs and not repeat mistakes.

She said she was afraid of planes and I explained that I used to be, but now I look at the people waiting to board the plane and the energy and ask if these people are going to die today. When I get the answer no, I feel safe.

It is similar to seeing that matrix. There are no flat out victims who are in the wrong place at the wrong time. There are choices to live what we need to in order to learn what we need to.

- - -

In life there are always repeating patterns; opportunities to get it right. The thing is to make those loops spiral. Tape loops that just replay don't resolve karma.

There have been times when I have had feelings that I'm finally fed up and I'm seeking a missing link in myself. I've begun to suspect that this link is in the way of my honesty, purity, and true wholesomeness. I have felt that it goes back to patterns that are deep in the past. I've felt like I'm chickening out on my power.

The search for the missing link is the search for whatever it is that it takes to make the process spiral and not loops.

- - -

I had this realization during a time of extraordinary rhythm in my life. From my journals:

> I have sometimes wondered where my rewards
> are and after doing good deeds have wondered how
> or when I would get rewarded. I have been many
> many times the good Samaritan, but feel that I have
> reaped very few rewards for it. Where is my good
> karma? What I realized is that that way of looking
> for rewards has been transcended. I now feel aware
> that free of history and living in unity, events that
> might have been labeled successes or failures or

might have been considered rewards are simply all part of the same matrix. And as far as the question, where is my good karma? It is not to be found as an end result. The more I live in unity, the more I am one with events and with my fellow beings, then what might have been seen as rewards before are now simply recognized as facets of what I think of as "my life."

Two years later, during a time when I felt that my faith was very high and that my acts were part of a spiritual reality which I all too often forget (no, not forget intellectually; forget in the core of my being, while being swept along in daily life surrounded by the paradigm of hard work for hard results) I was aware of a similar cosmic reality.

I observed how my acts of kindness, my "good karma" acts seemed to be supporting my ether, as it were. Often, in the past, when I'd wondered where the repayment was, there was an attitude of cynicism and separation. Like, "pay up universe."

Imagine raising a kid that way. "Let's see if you can do this. I'll bet you can't," along with the cynical vibe. Pretty bad.

But what I was feeling was not a "re-action" from the universe, rather I was seeing my acts resulting in good feelings in me that supported my ability to project myself such that I encountered a kind world.

It's so subtle, but it seems like a curious paradoxical place of power that at once is life created by me and life simply lived and participated in by me.

- - -

Everything you do or think or intend becomes a part of you, as well as a part of the whole; the god we all are. The earth is a place of doing; it's where doing really matters. That's really the whole point. Hard physical doing creates results that are often irreversible. It could be physical harm or it could be to set a course of action rolling that will lead to a change for the worse. Such doing, such actions create karma. Which means it's not consequence free for the doer.

Thoughts and intentions do have consequences, within and without, but in a less dramatic sense. Thoughts and intentions affect the ether and they can be felt as vibrations, like perhaps the mood in a room or at a gathering of folks. But in this realm, subtler than the hard physical doing, there is a lot of room to change your vibrations, and "make good" without apparent long term consequences.

In any case, acts out of harmony indicate that the doer is not in harmony within themselves, and therefore they must in some way be thrust again into a situation to get it right.

One of the great misunderstandings about karma, however, is that it is all about what we do to others; it is also what we do to ourselves. When we hurt others, we have chosen the low road and stepped off of the high road to heaven. It is our own well being that is compromised. The act out of harmony causes tension, affects your blood flow and pressure and adds friction to the full energetic system that you are. It is awkwardness where there should be ease. It is heavy where there should be light. And it is an entanglement of the future and the past where there should be free sailing.

- - -

Personally, I use the words "bad karma" and "good karma", but mostly as convenience to simplify and to avoid going into the nuances. And, although there are many nuances, there is some truth to the concept of and really no harm in most of the time just thinking of karma as good or bad. However, considering the nuances, there really is no "bad" karma. Bad karma compels us to be thrust into situations where we must learn a lesson that we had an opportunity to learn and failed, so that we have another chance. In that sense it's good. It's bad in the sense that it may be very undesirable or uncomfortable. It often involves such things as having to walk a mile in the shoes, so to speak, of another being that was hurt by our actions.

And as far as "good" karma goes, I would say good karma is when we act in such a way that it supports, encourages, and helps bring about unity, both for ourselves within and consequently for the whole and the greater good and health of the whole. It is harmonious. Good karma doesn't compel repetition of lessons to be learned, rather it is "rewarded" by ease, harmony, and good feelings. And this is what I call grace.

I used the word "compel" in describing bad karma. Somehow the universe, with us in complicity, compels us to learn somehow the lesson failed to be learned before. In grace, we play a more active role in the choices of future situations we will find ourselves in along our path.

Each time we return to earth physically for another sojourn, we return with "good" and "bad" karma. As we refine our self and become more in harmony, grace tends to play a bigger role and we are less compelled and choose more ease. The lessons become gentler.

- - -

Having said what I said above about being compelled to learn the lessons we failed before, I would like to add that I believe it doesn't necessarily have to be a long trudging road as we refine ourselves. I believe that a lifetime of karma can be erased with a thought. I haven't seen much evidence of that on such a scale but I have experienced within myself and observed in others the ability to let go to harmony, superseding something that might have compelled a karmic response. Though it does seem to be more in our nature to struggle and to let go of small pieces of our baggage a little at a time I do not believe there is a rule that we have to struggle. Redemption is a powerful tool.

- - -

Finally, I can't feel that I'm done with the karma and grace theme without addressing the death penalty.

The death penalty is first of all just plain barbaric. The only reason for the death penalty is for revenge. Fact of the matter is that those who wish it, support it, or do it, and especially those who revel in it, incur a great deal of heavy karma.

Among other things, one thing the death penalty does is that it denies the person a chance to redeem themselves, no matter what crime they have committed. If allowed to live, they are granted the opportunity to find the place where they were out of harmony and to come to a place within themselves where they can heal that aspect of their karma. Redemption is not an act done so you can say I did public service or did time and paid my dues and now I'm cleansed. It is something more of the heart and soul. Coming to a place of real knowing within. There are no guarantees that any individual will do this but when a person is denied this opportunity, it isn't just bad for them, it hurts everyone. It leaves an open wound and we all will pay in some way for that lost opportunity to have that wound healed.

One of my favorite themes in the original Star Trek series was redemption and belligerent beings returning to the fold. There were many episodes in which warring people (I say people for simplicity's sake) or people who had done great harm or committed heinous acts were forgiven in the end. Out in space Kirk was not forced to obey a law written in stone; he was allowed his judgment. And many who committed "criminal" acts weren't punished once it was clear that misunderstandings and injustices were recognized and those who had committed the misdeeds had made peace within and now felt it to be one with the community. Kirk was able to recognize the redemption and the opportunity to welcome a new friend and confidently allowed these people a chance to start over on a new higher path.

Of course that was fiction and very idealistic but still, I believe, something for us, both personally and as a society, to strive for as much as we can.

The Golden Rule Dilemma

Do unto others as you would have them do unto you. It sounds simple enough, on the surface. I have respected it as a truly admirable cornerstone of the best of the Christian tenets. Then it occurred to me that it has really been a player in many of the dilemmas I have faced. And it is, in its purest essence, really very controversial.

I have looked into the golden rule equivalent in other religions. They all have their own versions but most are similar. Some take a negative approach. Don't do unto others what you would not have them do unto you. It seemed to me, based on the translations and realizing that they are of other cultures, to the best of my understanding, that they are all equally oversimplified and controversial.

Following are some thoughts relative to this.

- - -

I want to be able to expect a lot from people and I put it on friends.

In the purest sense of doing to others what you would have them do to you, I have often disturbed and enraged people, because I would have people challenge me, tell me how they see it and be open and forward.

For example, I do wish my friends could and would be happy. But I think for me, how I wish it or show it is so different. It seems to me that mostly when people wish happiness on or for friends, it is a kind of pure, simple, wish. Just be happy. I think that is hard for me to do in a similar manner because invariably I see so much that I feel they need to undo before they can be happy and that undoing becomes part of the wish; part of my best intentions' wish for them. Maybe they could even be what they call happy but it's hard for me to wish that on them. The dilemma here is that what I would wish that they would do unto me is to challenge me to face issues in order to be happy. I would wish that they would want to help me change. Yet if I do that unto them, without explicit permission, more often than not it would be unwanted.

Interesting question. Should one recognize others' resistance and be honest only to a point, staying in realms comfortable to them, allowing, or should one really do unto others?

So, let me offer this addition to the golden rule. It is the way in which you are true and straight in doing unto others. Are you harsh or soft; attacking or cultivating? Maybe the "do" unto others is the problem. Maybe it should be more like "while doing unto others be sure to nurture them as you would want to be nurtured."

- - -

In the Evil theme I talked about the big discussion that I had with a couple of people I knew about laws and licensing massage; they were defending required licenses and a small group of people's right to legislate their ethics and I was simply saying, what can be wrong with adults deciding to do anything peaceful together with no victims. They defended their view saying it wasn't the government who decided the rules; it was a group of massage therapists.

As far as their side goes, for all of their benevolent dictator attitude, were they also acting with the golden rule? Did they prefer being told by authorities what not to do, simplifying their lives? And therefore did they feel it was also in my best interest to be controlled, and doing unto me would be to control me? There is the rub.

- - -

At Harbin Hot Springs there is an area with a number of small decks for camping. When there once I had some tension with a woman on the next deck over about my taking over a deck that has some stuff on it but seemed to me to be unused; the few items seemed abandoned. She told me she didn't think I should use the deck. I suggested using the deck and graciously yielding it if someone were to show up saying it was theirs. She told me that was a really male pushy thing to do. She wanted Harbin security to ok the take over, which, of course, pushed my buttons.

Afterwards, it occurred to me that both of us had been using the golden rule.

With all good intent and hopes to ease the tension, I went back later and expressed to her my thoughts, suggested that we were both just doing what we thought was best, and about us both using the golden rule. She was grim and uptight and seemed to refuse to find any common ground we could come to.

I guess that was just an escalation of the first failing of the golden rule. For me, doing unto her was to attempt to make peace so we could live happily ever after. For her, doing unto others; what she would expect from me, was to leave it alone regardless of the unresolved tension. And to relegate the resolution to Authority.

A possible golden rule interpretation: maybe it's not the physical act, but the intention. If I do unto others it might be very disturbing. Perhaps instead temper, tailor the act to achieve my intent; an act they appreciate.

But that's tricky. That means I'm guessing about them.

- - -

Once I was thinking about pleasure and how it is so distorted in the world. How people get pleasure from things that hurt others or disturb others. A picture came to me of two people together affecting each other, each creating, imparting vibrations that bring pleasure to the other as well as themselves. But what about the sadist and masochist? This is where the golden rule breaks down big time.

The golden rule has to be modified somehow to call upon the people of the world to seek within for the goodness that wants all participants to share in the highest potential of pleasure and well being.

- - -

There was an article in a Peace Pilgrim Newsletter that told about a lawyer, inspired by Peace Pilgrim's book, Steps Toward Inner Peace, to work with other lawyers to mediate for the parties involved instead for fighting to win. He refers to the golden rule of dispute resolution: "Have it be your purpose to resolve the dispute rather than to gain advantage."

On a more etheric level the following is similar to this idea of not gaining advantage. I sometimes catch myself thinking unkind things about people. It came to me that there is a difference between thinking unkind thoughts and being aware of what's unpleasant or disturbing or distasteful. It's perfectly fine and even desirable to be aware of vibrations that feel unharmonious but it is something else altogether to be away from a situation and to continue to generate unkind thoughts or blame or judge. The latter binds everyone to a rigid psychic event. The former, being a proper use of awareness, then letting it go, can free us and allow all parties the psychic freedom we all need to improve ourselves and our lives.

This is a form of the golden rule for sure. And a pure one without catches.

- - -

In conclusion, I would say hear the words of the golden rule but modify it constantly and dynamically for each and every situation with the ultimate intent being to soften each others lives and nurture each other and promote equality and justice.

Imagination

Regarding the romance I wanted in my life but seemed unable to have, a friend was getting on my case, telling me it was just that I didn't believe I could have it. I got angry. Angry being challenged with the responsibility of creating my own outward physical reality.

Later, reflecting on it, it came to me so clearly.

I believe I'm healthy. My imaginings of health are strong.

Part of me believes I can have women and sex. But my shadow side says no. And in this case, its imagining is stronger.

There have been times of confidence and times when I've been validated from without when I could easily imagine having a fruitful romantic life but when encountering a disappointment, I let my shadow imaginings take over. It was not a lack of imagining my desires fulfilled; just a stronger imagining of being unsuccessful in that area of life. When there were difficulties in a relationship either I was a victim (read, fell victim to my shadow imaginings) or I neatly avoided imagining my ability to play a strong active role in a failing relationship and know my power to imagine us changing and growing.

Looking back I see that during those times of happiness and satisfaction I had good opportunities, with the confidence and validation, to seek out the roots of and challenge my shadow imaginings. When things go well is when you really have opportunities to recreate your patterns.

- - -

That example is about me personally, but I think it is a good one, because I doubt that it is unique to me and because it is really just about the levels of imagining and their interplay.

This from my journals regarding a woman I desired:

I was phantasizing us being together and her yielding to me. It was such a down energy. Why not imagine she might enjoy and desire loving me? In her own way and her own time. Since I can't control her anyway, this frees me of trying to manipulate her imaginings. Only that there's love out there and I can imagine my love might be desired. All I can expect is to be as close to someone or as compatible with someone as their imaginings allows them to be with me.

We all have karma and bring tendencies into each life, but they are only tendencies. It's not that we are forever affected by such influences and consequently live our lives as we do. It is simply that we; our faith, our positive, beneficial, happy imaginings are challenged and God and the Devil have their playground on earth.

But we have free will and we can create through imagining conditions that are beneficial. In fact, that is the reason we come back; to lessen that karma and work towards grace and play a more constructive role for ourselves and all concerned. And I think that is exactly why we're here. To imagine beauty when history tells us life or the world is ugly.

- - -

Imagining is at its best when it isn't a completely cerebral act. It is best accompanied by a unified heart. A solid sense of how we would like it, ourselves, and it all to be. A commitment to your heart's desire. Never allow your ego and your mind's hunger for center stage intimidate what your heart and gut tell you. It's helpful to develop this and be freed of trying to orchestrate results. If you can cultivate a unified heart in harmony with your imagining, then there is really no figuring you need to do.

There's really no acting or way of acting or particular course of action that is required. To do so is like treating the symptom. Working at changing acts is working backwards.

The acts, the sense, the logic, will follow as a result of winning the challenge of the imagination.

- - -

OK. Now let's go one step further. It's clear that we can't just go around imagining whatever we want and it will all come true. We share this world with many other beings who also have the power of imagining. So let's say I can imagine peace but someone else can imagine war. All of what I've already said is still true but as a community, as a unit, as parts of a whole, it hangs in the balance of our individual imaginings.

My imaginings can't make anybody else do or believe anything or make them want me or make them decide anything favorable towards me. But my imaginings makes me a vital participant and a responsible creator as does everyone else's.

It might seem at first that someone selfish, greedy, or power hungry would simply choose dominance and have it free of retribution, but that's not the case. In group and community dynamics there are combinations of imagining. There are infinite gradations of both imaginings with little impact on other beings and imaginings with great impact on other beings. If one person's imaginings impact another's comfort and "well-being" then there is conflict. With free will and the complexity of our desires it can get messy. That's where commonality comes in. If groups of beings having similar ideals and desires can combine their wills and imaginings, they will have more influence. One can only hope that the desire we all have for the health of the world is greater than the desire for dominance over others.

- - -

And we, us humans, are not alone here. I believe that accepting or assuming that all things, the rocks, the weather, the planets are all a part of a greater whole, they would all share the power of imagining. And it would explain the relationships of all things and their unique vibrations contributing in their unique ways to our combined imagining and the consequent creating of the world and the universe as we know it.

We, as more conscious beings, however, having a greater power of imagination, with a long reach, therefore carry more responsibility to use our free will to achieve harmony. We need to recognize and honor the (s)lower beings who are "happy" with less demands in space and time. Rocks aren't that picky. There is much flexibility in imagining relationships with a rock without it dynamically affecting the community.

Also there are slower vibrating beings - trees for example – who may not extend as far in their imagining as other beings individually, but a forest or planetary community of trees and their unity with weather, water, etc. does compel a level of natural law to be reckoned with.

- - -

I'll finish this theme with some thoughts on the power of imagining over history and sequential life.

- - -

We must recognize and believe that our history isn't our fate. It's simply that there are times when our guard is down and we lose the faith and imagine the worst or at least imagine less than we desire. Be certain of this; our history isn't proof of any pattern beyond our completely self fulfilling prophesy.

From my journals:

> During my run that I just got back from I was thinking about the traps of sequential acts. It occurred to me that there are physical limitations. Like I'm in the same body that historically took a

couple of months to develop solid running shape. Then I decided to change that to physical "predispositions." As a spirit we have chosen our body, our astrology, our others to gather together with, and we have made our contracts with ourselves. But all of this is only our predisposition. We are free agents. We decide ultimately what choices we will make, regardless of the volume and intensity of the committee voices; each with their own agenda.

Tonight I feel like I'm mustering my courage to blow my life apart. I mean to blow apart the linear conservative sequence, safely chosen to accommodate patterns of behavior that appear falsely to be wisdom. And to shed society's idea of sanity; a safe sequential predictable course. Normal and utterly perverse.

- - -

I have noticed that whenever I move or I'm in a new place where people don't know me that I have an opportunity to kind of start over. I don't feel as timid to do nutty things that normally make me feel self conscious. Once I feel people know me, I get the feeling that it's harder to act differently. I feel the energy of their thinking, "wow, this is out of character." There is a word in German, Narrenfreiheit, which means fool's freedom. Yeah. The fool's freedom that we all should have. And not just to feel nutty, but much more importantly to break the threads of limitations and to break out of our little boxes.

- - -

In conversation with a friend of a roommate, he expressed his distaste for people asking what he did, meaning work, etc. I said make up tales. Spin a fanciful yarn. Cloak it all and have fun. The truth is that anyone worth their salt would know more about you from your foolishness and spontaneous creativity than from any list of life facts.

- - -

I once saw a movie that was a beautiful example of the power of overcoming the hold of sequential life. It was called "Another Woman" with Justine Bateman. She had lost her memory. She finds herself in a relationship with a loving caring man (her husband) who doesn't trust her. They essentially start over, she being now sweet and loving, the sequence of her behavior in her crumbling marriage broken. She and her husband slowly rebuild trust and loving before she discovers the blame and unforgiving that had put distance between them the first time around; she now ready to let it go.

- - -

Yes, imagine yourself how and who you would like to be. Use your unified heart in concert with your imaginings. Try and not be limited by your sequential life and your history. When you are imagining, shuck all limitations. Imagine your dreams coming true. Remember, you can't and shouldn't try to override someone else's free will to engage in their own personal imagining. You can't have everything you want just by imagining, but you can shape yourself and your interactions for the most positive and highest quality possibilities.

Sensing, Feeling, Thinking

Be aware when engaging the mind. The mind is a great tool, but you should proceed with caution when it makes your decisions or dominates your behavior; particularly when communicating with others. Featuring logic or psychological thinking can severely hamper communications skills. The natural flow and timing can easily be overridden.

Live in your body.

Living in your head is not good. The head is meant to be visited. Unlike the body, there is no indoor plumbing to eliminate waste. When the mind is only visited it remains uncluttered so that fresh, creative, innovative thinking can be put to use. Sensory input is allowed to come in unmolested and will pass through beautifully. Old baggage, repeated thoughts, and old tape loops create dross and clog things up and will eventually seep into the body.

I'm sure there are people who believe that to live in the body is heathen and hedonistic; that the head is where intellect, logic, philosophy, belief, and values are to be found.

Yes, it is true that the reflective mind has its role, but all of those aspects of the mind are easily corrupted, hypnotized, co-opted and perverted. The qualities of truth and goodness and health and righteousness are things you feel in your heart, in your gut. And in your muscles.

The head predominant is insufficient and reckless at best, dangerous at worst.

- - -

There are those who believe that in order to get it all together and to seek to be part of the whole, the best way is to escape this plane and the physical. I call this cosmic escapism.

The irony is that the fastest way to get out of your body attachment is to get into your body. It is the body that holds us here and there is a reason for that. It's kind of like an apprenticeship. You have to learn to manage and run a body before you can move on.

- - -

There is a lot of misunderstanding about what I call inharmonious acts of passion, better know as bad deeds. People get into their head and when it directs and orchestrates all of the body's dramas, they think they're into their body. Then they think the body is the culprit. The body gets blamed. This is a shame.

This has resulted in a lot of puritanical attitudes that continue to screw up just about every culture on earth.

The body and emotions get a bad name because of the misunderstanding of how the process of denial and the mind's dis-ease compel inharmonious acts of passion. Inharmonious acts of passion are determined by a psychology, which is a (subconscious) mental choice to be selective as to what's believed from what's taken in from parent, bible, teachers, and the scientist.

Where does psychology come from, which is to say why do we selectively believe what we are "taught" or selectively believe what we experience? From needs not met. From holes needing to be filled and from the radar that screens out what is too challenging.

Why is it too challenging? Because we have limited our feelings and consequently our experiences and have fear of the unknown. Experience means allowing our surroundings and senses to affect us. That means really fully experiencing, not just "doing" something new that is physically new but that can be packaged neatly within certain parameters.

So it is the limiting of feelings and the limiting of sensing information and not the indulgence in them that starts the chain reaction that leads the mind to direct distorted acts.

- - -

While talking with a friend he said that one would hope that leaders would want to promote unity or something like that. I said to him that I believed that the reason that so many of our leaders are involved in politics and law is because they fear natural flow and need to support control and constraints.

He said he hoped the fear wouldn't bring them down to the animal level. Fact of the matter is, as I see it, that a person acting on fear and adding human ingenuity to it, extends below the animal level. I kind of see this picture of a pivot point of animal naiveté. With pureness of action (however much or lack thereof) and our intent tipping us above or below that level. It is not the physical animal that we are that is responsible but the intent that drives it. And that intent is vulnerable as a function of the mind. The body and the senses don't lie. They simply cannot. It is the head's interpretation that distorts the input.

- - -

I have always been very sensitive to noise, garish visual assaults, awful and toxic smells and so on. Many people have said to me, don't worry, you'll get used to it. I think it is a function of the mind to stop awareness of the body's messages if a choice has been made to continue to co-exist with some undesirable influence. It is a kind of survival mechanism. But it is also a trap. It is sometimes hard to realize that you've stopped sensing or feeling something because of a "good reason" but now that reason has passed. So you continue being numb.

What a cheat of our senses and body information.

Similarly, I have noticed that sometimes when I experience something and I am not satisfied with what I feel, I will seek to control the situation by explaining it. Once I've explained it, that can tend to limit the sensory and feeling input. The mind's reasoning based on sensory and feeling input must be fluid. Labeling and attaching finality to something can close the book on it, when there is, for sure, so much more of the story to be told.

- - -

Society teaches us to use speech to share experience. It also attempts to teach us to inhibit the body and emotions so as to not "reflect" experience. But the body must and will, as a creature of nature, reflect experience. Speech becomes a substitute used all too often as a contrived tool dedicated to communicating experience in common or traditional terms; a safer way to convey and share experience than allowing the body to express itself naturally and fully.

Children use their bodies freely to express themselves. If they are upset they might, for example, stomp their feet, tilt their head and scrunch up their face. We, society, as adults, feel it is out of line to make a scene. We fall back on words. This is not only unfortunate because we fail to communicate fully but also because in the process we lose the ability to truly read what another is communicating to us. Certainly we all read body language to some extent, but it is severely limited.

Also, anytime we choose to inhibit the body's reflecting of our inner feelings, there is a physical price to pay. If the body's natural response is not allowed full expression, it will be manifested as tension or stress somewhere within the body.

- - -

Emotions function as signals. If you hold on to any emotion because of a mental attachment or for ulterior motives, then there may not be a place for another emotion to surface to show your true response to new thoughts or conditions. Try to not crystallize, categorize, or package your emotions. This will allow new unobstructed emotions to surface and be fully experienced and then yield to new ones.

This exception, from my journals:

When I was questioning the role of emotions and suggesting they could pass after having shown us what prompted them, I wondered about love and contented emotion and sustaining beautiful desirable emotions. Right now I feel that by learning from and respecting the lessons of the emotions that arise, they will pass, however it could be possible to maintain an underlying contented non-dramatic love. And the way I feel right now, I would also say my love is not directed. People that shine in my presence are recognized warmly but it's not because of or for them I feel this love. I believe that there is a kind of pure love that could be sustained without needing to yield in order to allow the free flow of new emotions.

- - -

And the following is a journal entry from a time when I was living in Santa Cruz, a California beach town, that offers some thought regarding the power of the mind over the body and how it can get "hung up" rather than letting go and allowing something to pass:

Today I drove by the market across the street from Teva's at 41st and Portola and remembered the time I was in there and a woman was in there wearing a small bikini and how much it excited me, especially being away from the beach.

I found it very curious and revelatory to realize that if I had seen her yesterday, dressed in the same bikini, when I was at the hot springs where everybody was naked, it probably wouldn't have left such an impression. And yet, although I'm in a different state now, the original charge and impulse are still there. "Impression" is a good word for it.

It's not even "me" now but I still feel, with this memory, the titillation and uneasiness and the feelings of yearning and incompleteness. I feel it now, even as I write, in my nerves, in my arms. Quite amazing how a mere memory, having no reality in the present can continue to generate its original impulse. And it seems that it takes more spiritual work and conviction and knowing to pacify that charge imprinted in my body, than it does a similar event in physical reality in the present. It seems to me that this theme deserves attention. Maybe I need to reword, re-edit the memory. Not the memory, actually. I think it is good to allow it to be, but to disengage the tendrils still wrapped around my nervous system.

It's like how sometimes when in a state of grace you can still observe the flotsam and jetsam of your past trials and tribulations without being affected by them. I think it would be healthy to use those times to address past entanglements and to try and allow them and their charge to pass.

- - -

I have given some thought to the three possible orders in which people think, feel, and act. For each individual there must be many variables depending on circumstances and on one's past history in similar situations. People probably have predominate patterns but vary them with conditions and how secure they are, and other factors. For example, faced with a critical choice, thinking first would often be wise. Under attack I might act first. With a lover under soft lights I might feel first, let that guide my actions, and minimize and put thinking on a back burner.

I think we could all learn a lot about ourselves by observing the order in which we think, feel and act.

- - -

In conclusion let me say this. The dynamics of sensing, feeling, and thinking is truly mind boggling. Which is exactly why we should live in the body. Somewhere under our confusions, the body is telling us the truth.

About the Author

I was born in Seattle and spent the first 30 years of my life in the Pacific Northwest. Well, except for 4 school years in a private Quaker boarding school in Pennsylvania, which was a great communal living experience. I think this had a far reaching and profound effect on my life. I have since lived in many different places, mostly favoring the West Coast; Olympia, Bellingham, San Juan Island, San Luis Obispo, Santa Cruz, Santa Fe, Maui, Kauai and currently Sebastopol, California. Integral in my experience has been a number of trips to Europe, mostly spending my time in the area around Innsbruck, Austria, which is my second home and where I have so many dear friends.

Work has also been varied; most of it being for myself. I have worked as a carpenter and with a partner built 2 houses in the mountains (one in Idaho, one in Washington) using (almost) exclusively hand tools. In Santa Cruz, I started my own business building and selling portable massage tables of my own design and did that for many years.

I love music; my favorites being classical music of the more sublime nature (Debussy, for one) and psychedelic era rock of which I consider the Beatles to be the ultimate. My favorite instrument is the human voice. Music has been a cornerstone of my life and has carried me through many peaceful and turbulent times.

I love to get out and ramble around on my mountain bike. It keeps me young; not the exercise so much as the playfulness and freedom of it.

And my most recent passion is playing strategic eurogame board games with friends.

Check out my Smashwords author interview here:
https://www.smashwords.com/profile/view/Rogue17154

Other Books by Roger Golden Brown

The Truth Seeker's Handbook has been published in print and as an eBook. I kept journals for over 20 years, writing almost every day. Much of the philosophy, the struggles leading to learning and the attitudes that helped me get through life appears in this book. It has a section dealing with major life themes, one about our relationship to the Earth, one retelling stories of serendipity, and finally a section of reminders to help along the way. Reminders is one of the 4 sections that make up Truth Seeker's Handbook.

Excerpt from The Truth Seeker's Handbook:

> Delight in truth at all costs. We really must accept everything we experience. Simply say, yes, this is happening to me. We tend to avoid and repress and choose against less pleasant feelings. What a rip-off! They offer powerful information as to what is going on; information as to the reason why we don't at the moment have pleasant feelings. The desirable feelings validate flow and rightness. The unpleasant ones are the ones needing the most attention.

- - -

Insights has been published in print and as an eBook. This is a compilation of most of the journal entries which didn't appear in any of my other books, but that I felt needed to see the light of day. I organized them into such categories as Cosmic, Philosophy and Attitude, Love, Society, and several more.

Excerpt from Insights:

> I heard Earth Angel on the radio today and thought about the American Dream and its surfacing in the 50's and the dreamy songs reflecting it. I was overwhelmed with a rush of rightness. Sure it is distorted. Sure its means are destructive. But the dream - to have comfort and ease and the time and

space to relax and expand, time to create, to have comfortable homes is fine. It sparked a spiritual movement which unfortunately was complicated by an awesome opportunity to be corrupted by material and sensory numbing diversions. But the dream itself, it's not only the American Dream but a soul's dream. To mellow a life in a body. To find harmony. I'm all for it.

- - -

Heading Out is poetry and prose and has been published in print and as an eBook. Cryptic and cosmic might be good words to describe these writings; word adventures. Poetry is an individual thing and I can't say for sure you will like them, but look for it and check out the free eBook sample.

A short poem from Heading Out:

> Popsicle process brings freedom … in heat.
> What was ice yields a watery treat.
> When we allow ourselves to have what we need
> That water fertilizes and brings life to our seed.

- - -

Encounters has been published in print and as an eBook. It is about encounters with women in my life that were romantic and sometimes intimate but does not include the girlfriends or lovers of duration. It is all journal entries in real time; usually my initial feelings, the encounter evolving, and finally myself seeking resolution and completion for myself and hopefully us. These encounters took place mostly during my 20's and 30's and are very gutsy and emotional. I have been a very emotional person and it may surprise some people to read a man's feelings essentially unedited.

Excerpt from Encounters:

> I approached her during a thunderstorm downpour on the main sunning deck (at Harbin Hot Springs). I was attracted to her and felt an

immediate thrill from and affection for her. I wanted her. I spent some time with her and got to know her a little. I slept next to her on the sleeping deck. She let me know she needed space. She removed my hand gently from her body, but didn't let go. She held my hand a few moments more. What a beautiful softening of the space between us that she required. I was hurt and felt rejected, although I appreciated her communication and integrity. I cried. Strange sleep. Dreams. I felt again defeated but fought it, hung in there.

- - -

33 Years of Dreams has been published in print and as an eBook. Over a period of 33 years I wrote down a ton of dreams. A friend once said to me, why would anybody want to read anyone else's dreams? That got me to thinking but it came to me you could also ask why would anybody want to read anyone else's poetry? They are the same, in a way; kind of cryptic non-linear stories that take images and create something to be interpreted. After trimming out some of the uninteresting and poorly transcribed dreams it is, in its final form, almost 700 pages and is published in 2 volumes. They are for sale individually.

A dream from 33 Years of Dreams:

I was with a pet, female, smiling Buffalo and a group of friends hanging out in the country. And with an alien friend who materialized to be with us. There was a river scene, after going through a gate. Rednecks were hassling us, then we saw three of our women being physically abused down the road a ways, by three men. We headed down in force (with our alien and Buffalo) to deal with it.

Where to Buy the Books

To buy the books in print go to my Author Page:
http://books2read.com/rogergoldenbrown

Versions of these books in eBook format can all be found at
Smashwords, as well as free sample downloads:
https://www.smashwords.com/profile/view/Rogue17

Appreciation

A warm thank you and appreciation for all the friends that were there for me along the way. Especially Karin, Russ, Fred, Keith, my brother, mother, and father, George School, Santa Cruz, and all the water I have swum in.

Please contact me should you want to comment or ask about anything. Also I would appreciate any feedback if any typos are discovered.

wordsmith@goldengalaxies.net

Thanks for reading.